TOGETHER IN PRAYER

When You Pray
You Talk To God
When God Talks To You
Do You Listen?

DEDICATION

The path to Heaven is paves with bricks of prayer. The most notable bricks are surely formed by novenas to God's beloved friends in Heaven – the Saints and Holy Angels. This booklet contains some of the most popular, traditional novena prayers as well as other prayers and meditations. God is eager to hear our prayers – to grant us many favors, both spiritual and temporal. No petition is too great or too small for our all-loving God. Heaven is there for all of us – at the end of our "path of prayers."

MARY'S CALL

P.O. Box 162
504 W. U.S. Hwy. 24
Salisbury, MO 65281

Phone: 660-388-5308
Email: maryscall@maryscall.com

www.maryscall.com

MARY'S CALL

Mary's Call is a small, not-for-profit family organization. Our ministry is to encourage prayer, especially the Rosary and Way of the Cross.

The original undertaking of Mary's Call was the production of a 15 decade Rosary tape with meditations plus six hymns. The first order for the tape was received on May 4, 1989 (Ascension Thursday).

We create Mary's Call unique books and have available bibles, rosaries, scapulars, religious books, plaques, and many other items and religious gifts. In order for items to be sold at the lowest price, every effort is made to keep production costs to a minimum and, at the same time, maintain exceptional standards.

Mary's Call remains a very small family organization and is able to operate only through the assistance (time, talent, and donations) of friends. We hope that you will receive many blessings as a result of joining us in this ministry of prayer.

TABLE OF CONTENTS

YOU NEED TO PRAY!..8

A POWERFUL PRAYER TO BE SAID BEFORE
PRAYING...9

O JESUS 9

GOD'S WILL 10

PEACE PRAYER 10

A PRAYER FOR TODAY 11

A HEALING PRAYER...15

WHY CALLEST THOU ME?......................................16

LOVE ISN'T LOVE TILL YOU GIVE IT AWAY ...17

LOVELY LADY...18

ONLY A LITTLE WHILE 19

PRAYER FOR DIRECTION 20

A TEENAGER'S CREED..21

JELLYBEAN PRAYER...21

IN THANKSGIVING FOR A FAVOR RECEIVED .22

INDIFFERENCE 23

FORGIVENESS PRAYER...24

TO THE BLESSED VIRGIN 25

FOR THE ELDERLY 25

HAPPINESS 26

HOLY WATER 27

OTHERS..28

PHILOSOPHY OF LIFE..30

MEDITATION 31

THERE'S A REASON 31

IF GOD SHOULD GO ON STRIKE........................ 32

BE SATISFIED 33

GOD'S BOUQUET 34

PRAYER FOR A FAMILY 35

YOU ARE LOVED 36

ADORATION 37

PRAYER FOR THE DEAD.................................. 38

A PRAYER FOR THOSE GROWING OLD 39

ST. GERTUDE THE GREAT NOVENA 40

PRAYER OF ST. GERTRUDE THE GREAT 40

TO THE HOLY SOULS IN PURGATORY 41

NOVENA PRAYER TO ST. PHILOMENA............. 42

TO ST. PEREGRINE "THE CANCER SAINT"....... 44

PRAYER TO ONE'S PATRON OR ANY SAINT ... 45

THE BEST THINGS IN LIFE ARE FREE 45

TO ST. MICHAEL THE ARCHANGEL 46

TO ST. RAPHAEL THE ARCHANGEL.................. 47

TO GOOD ST. ANNE...................................... 48

PRAYER TO ST. ANTHONY............................... 49

TO ST. GERARD... 50

For an expectant Mother 50

TO ST. GERARD... 51

TO ST. DYMPHNA 52

TO ST. MARY GORETTI 53

TO ST. THERESE OF THE CHILD JESUS, "THE LITTLE FLOWER" 53

TO THE HOLY ANGELS 54

NOVENA TO ST. JOSEPH 55

TO OUR LADY OF PERPETUAL HELP.................56

PRAYER TO ST. PIUS X.......................................57

NOVENA OF GRACE IN HONOR OF ST. FRANCIS XAVIER 57

NOVENA TO ST. RITA 58

TO OUR LADY OF LOURDES 59

TO ST. BENEDICT 60

TO ST. ANTHONY MARY CLARET......................61

PRAYER TO BE SAID BY A SICK PERSON 62

IN HONOR OF THE SORROWSOF THE BLESSSED VIRGIN MARY 63

TO ST. LUCY 64

TO ST. JUDE THE APOSTLE...............................64

NOVENA OF CONFIDENCE TO THE SACRED HEART 65

NOVENA PRAYERS TO OUR LADY OF THE SNOWS 66

NOVENA IN URGENT NEED TO THE INFANT JESUS OF PRAGUE...67

THE BOOK OF LIFE! 69

GREAT THOUGHTS.................................... 70

YOUR CROSS 71

ANGEL'S PRAYER.................................... 72

"HONOR THY FATHER…"..................................... 73

THE HEART OF CHRIST 74

THE LEGEND OF THE DOGWOOD...................... 75

STAYING CLOSE TO JESUS 76

LORD, TAKE MY WILL............................. 77

A PRAYER TO REDEEM LOST TIME.................... 77

YOU NEED TO PRAY!

Because we do not see the value of prayer, we say we have no time for prayer.

FIRST, we need to pray, because our salvation depends on it.

St. Alphonsus Ligouri said: "If I had only one sermon to preach, I'd preach it on prayer." "For," he said, "if you pray, you will be saved; if you do not pray you will be lost."

Someone put it this way in rhyme:

> If you pray well, you'll live well.
> If you live well, you'll die well.
> If you die well, you won't go to hell.
> And if you don't go to hell, then all is well.

The plight of the world today and the victories of Satan in the world can be attributed to the single fact that we are relying too much on our own resources — ourselves, our sciences, our technologies — and not at all on prayer.

A POWERFUL PRAYER TO BE SAID BEFORE PRAYING

"Almighty Father, I place the Precious Blood of Jesus before my lips before I pray, that my prayers may be purified before they ascend to Your divine altar."

-- St. Mary Magdalen de Pazzi

O JESUS

In union with your most precious blood poured out on the cross and offered in every mass, I offer you today my prayers, works, joys, sorrows and sufferings for the praise of Your holy name and all the desires of Your sacred heart; in reparation for sin, for the conversion of sinners, the union of all Christians and our final union with you in heaven.

GOD'S WILL

Dearest Lord, teach me to be generous; teach me to serve You as You deserve; to give and note to count the cost, to fight and not to heed the wounds, to toil and not to seek for rest, to labor and not to ask for reward except that of knowing I am doing Your will.

-- St. Ignatius Loyola

PEACE PRAYER

Lord, make me an instrument of Your peace. Where there is hatred, let me sow love.

Where there is injury, pardon. Where there is doubt, faith. Where there is despair, hope. Where there is darkness, light. And where there is sadness, joy.

O Divine Master, grant that I may not so much seek to be consoled, as to console; to be understood, as to under- stand; to be loved, as to love. For it is in giving that we receive, it is in pardoning that we are pardoned, and it is in dying that we are born to Eternal Life!

-- St. Francis

A PRAYER FOR TODAY

This is the beginning of a new day. God has given us this day to use as we will. We can waste it – or use it for good, but what we do today is important because we are exchanging a day of our life for it! When tomorrow comes, this day will be gone forever, leaving in its place something that we have traded for it. We want it to be gain, and not loss; good and not evil; success and not failure; in order that we shall not regret the price we have paid for it.

To fall in love with God is the
Greatest of all romances; to seek
Him, the greatest adventure, to find
Him, the greatest human achievement.

PRELUDE TO PRAYER

You do not have to be clever to please Me; all you have to do is want to love Me. Just speak to Me as you would anyone of whom you are very fond.

Are there any people you want to pray for? Say, their names to Me, and ask of Me as much as you like. I am generous, and know all their needs, but I want you to show your love for them and Me by trusting Me to do what I know is best.

Tell me about the poor, the sick, and the sinners, and if you have lost the friendship of affection of anyone, tell Me about that too.

Is there anything you want for your soul? If you like, you can write out a long list of all your needs, and come and read it to Me. Tell Me of the things you feel guilty about. I will forgive you if you will accept it.

Just tell Me about your pride, your touchiness, self-centeredness, meanness and laziness. I still love you in spite of these. Do not be ashamed; there are many saints in heaven who had the same faults as you; they prayed to Me, and little by little, their faults were corrected.

Do not hesitate to ask Me for blessings for the body and mind; for health, memory, and success. I can give everything, and I always do give everything needed to make souls holier for those who truly want it.

What is it that you want today? Tell Me, for I long to do you good. What are your plans? Tell Me about them. Is there anyone you want to please?

What do you want to do for them?

And don't you want to do anything for Me? Don't you want to do a little good to the souls of your friends who perhaps have forgotten Me? Tell Me about your failures, and I will show you the cause of them. What are your worries? Who has caused you pain? Tell Me all about it and add that you will forgive, and be kind to him, and I will bless you.

Are you afraid of anything? Have you any tormenting, unreasonable fears? Trust yourself to Me. I am here. I see everything. I will not leave you.

Have you no joys to tell Me about? Why do you not share your happiness with Me? Tell Me what has happened since yesterday to cheer and comfort you. Whatever it was, however big, however small, I prepared it. Show Me your gratitude and thank Me.

Are temptations bearing heavily upon you? Yielding to temptations always disturbs the peace of your soul. Ask Me, and I will help you overcome them. Well, go along now. Get on with your work or play, or other interests. Try to be quieter, humbler, more submissive, kinder; and come back soon and bring Me a more devoted heart. Tomorrow I shall have more blessings for you.

When Jesus of Nazareth was harassed, tortured and condemned to death of the cross, He gave us an example to follow when we are hurting, in despair, in trouble and discomfort. From Our Lord's suffering, He provided the means for our salvation – by His death He guaranteed it.

Most of us do not knowingly or willingly subject ourselves to pain and suffering, but Jesus, Our Lord did.

Most of us shy away from making hard choices and decisions that may not be popular, but Chris, the Lord did.

And many of us are timid and afraid to make sacrifices for the benefit of another, but Jesus loves us so much that He subjected Himself to a cruel crucifixion as a means of showing us the way to happiness and peace.

So it is important that in times of difficulties, pain and suffering, we should turn in confidence to Our Merciful Lord, Who is well acquainted with our situation. Place yourself in His care and devoutly say: "Jesus, I trust in You."

A HEALING PRAYER

O Jesus, Good Shepherd,
You heal the sick and the needy
And comfort all those who mourn
Look kindly on me today and heal me,
Restore me to strength of soul and body,
And grant me Your loving gift of peace.

WHY CALLEST THOU ME?

Carved by an unknown sculptor, into the walls of an old European Cathedral, this appeal expresses the grief of Christ.

Thou callest Me MASTER...
yet heedest not Me,
Thou callest Me LIGHT...
yet I shine not in thee.
Thou callest Me WAY...
but dost follow Me not,
Thou callest Me LIFE...
yet My Name is forgot.
Thou callest me TRUTH...
But playest a false role,
Though callest Me GUIDE...
yet despisest control.
Thou callest Me LOVING...
withholding thy heart,
Thou callest Me RICH...
yet desirest no part.
Thou callest Me GOOD...
and yet evil thy ways,
Thou callest Me ETERNAL...
while wasting thy days.
Thou callest Me NOBLE...
yet draggest Me down,
Thou callest me MIGHTY...
yet fearing My frown.
Thou callest Me JUST...
Oh! If just then I be,
When I shall condemn thee,
reproach thou not Me.

16

LOVE ISN'T LOVE TILL YOU GIVE IT AWAY

One evening, just before the great star Mary Martin was to go on stage in *South Pacific* on Broadway, a note was handed to her. It was from Oscar Hammerstein, one of the authors of *South Pacific*, who at that moment was on his deathbed.

The short, vibrant note read: "Dear Mary, a Bell's not a bell till you ring it. A song's not a song till you sing it. Love in your heart was not put there to stay. Love isn't love till you give it away."

After Mary's performance that night, many people rushed backstage to congratulate her. They said, "Mary, you did something to us tonight. What was it?"

Blinking back the tears, Mary Martin read them the note. Then she said, "Tonight I gave my love away!"

Love is action! It isn't passive. The gift of our Father's love to us was His only Son, Jesus, who took our place on the cross…loving us that we might love…giving to us that we might give.

17

LOVELY LADY

Lovely Lady, dressed in blue,
Teach me how to pray.
God was just your little Boy –
Tell me what to say!
Did you lift Him up sometimes
Gently on your knee?
Did you sing to Him the way
Mother did to me?
Did you hold His hand at night?
Did you ever try
Telling stories of the world?
Oh! And did He cry?
Do you think He really cares
If I tell Him things –
Little things that happen? And
Do the Angels' wings
Make a noise? And can He hear
Me if I speak low?
Does He understand me now?
Tell me, for you know!
Lovely Lady, dressed in blue,
Teach me how to pray –
He was just your little Boy,
And you know the way.

                    -- Mary Dixon Thayer

ONLY A LITTLE WHILE

Only a little while, He saith,
    Only a little while;
A few more days, or a few more years,
A few more cares and smiles and tears;
At the longest 'twill seem but a fleeting breath,
    Only a little while.
Only a little while, He saith,
    Only a little while;
Dark clouds may enshroud us; rugged and steep
Be the path we tread; we may wearily weep;
But courage, my soul, for the Leader saith,
    Only a little while,
Only a little while, He saith,
    Only a little while.
A little while here with the pain and the cross,
A little while here to be purged from our dross;
And then, oh! The glory beyond that, He saith,
    Beyond this little while.
Oh! The crowns and the palms and the victorious song.
Oh! The joys, the glad raptures of glorified throngs,
The unknown, the unspeakable glories that await
    After this little while.

                        -- Rev. H.M. Calmer, S.J.

19

PRAYER FOR DIRECTION

Lord God, it is not clear to me
how I should spend my life.
It is not clear to me,
the way I should go.

I am often confused,
So many attractive things
hold out empty promises for happiness.

Help me through the prayers of
Saint John Bosco, who helped so many
young to find their way in life.

Help me to know your will for me,
and give me the courage to follow.

May I know the true joys
that are only found
in doing what is right and
giving my life for others
in Your Name.

Amen

A TEENAGER'S CREED

It's not enough to have a dream,
unless I'm willing to pursue it.
It's not enough to know what's right,
unless I'm strong enough to do it.

It's not enough to join the crowd,
to be acknowledged and accepted.
I must be true to my ideals,
even if I'm excluded and rejected.

It's not enough to learn the truth,
unless I also learn to live it.
It's not enough to reach for love,
unless I care enough to give it.

JELLYBEAN PRAYER

RED is for the blood He gave,
GREEN is for the grass HE made.
YELLOW is for HIS sun so bright,
ORANGE is for the edge of night.
BLACK is for the sins we made,
WHITE is for the grace HE gave.
PURPLE is for HIS hours of sorrow,
PINK is for our new tomorrow.

A bag full of jellybeans,
Colorful and sweet,
IS a prayer!
IS a promise!
IS a child's treat!

21

IN THANKSGIVING FOR A FAVOR
RECEIVED

Thank You, O God, for hearing my prayer and granting my request. Thank You for all the kindness You have shown me.

Thank You, Father, for Your great love in giving me my life, for Your great patience in preserving me despite my sinfulness, for Your protection in the past and for the opportunity to serve and honor You in the future.

Thank You, Lord Jesus, for keeping me numberless times for sin and death by the toils of Your life, the sufferings of Your Passion, and by Your victorious Resurrection.

Thank You, Holy Spirit of God for bestowing so many graces upon my soul and for having so frequently renewed Your life within me.

May my life, from now on, by a sign of my gratefulness. Amen.

INDIFFERENCE

When Jesus came to Golgotha
        they hanged Him on a tree,
They drove great nails through
        hands and feet and made a Calvary.
They crowned Him with a crown of thorns;
        red were His wounds and deep,
For those were crude and cruel days,
        and human flesh was cheap.
When Jesus came to AMERICA
        they only let Him die;
For men had grown more tender,
        and they would not give Him pain,
They only just passed down the street,
        and left Him in the rain.
Still Jesus cried: "Forgive them
        for they know not what they do,"
And still it rained the winter rain
        that drenched Him through and through.
The crowds went home and
        left the streets without a soul to see.
And Jesus crouched against a wall
        and Cried For Calvary!

It has been said that the greatest suffering Jesus experienced, was the knowledge that so much of His bitter passion, agony, and shedding of His Precious Blood would be wasted and in vain, because so many souls would reject His love and mercy, and the salvation He came to purchase for them at such great price. Let us never be cold or indifferent to Jesus, but let us be grateful for His love, and constantly implore His mercy for ourselves and for all poor sinners.

23

FORGIVENESS PRAYER

Jesus,
I really do believe that You are the Son of God
        And the Son of Mary, the true Christ.
Who came into the world to save sinners.
And I admit that I am a sinner,
        And that I need You.
Because without You I would have
        Been damned and lost forever.
So, with Mary as My Mother and Teacher,
I want to magnify You as my Lord
        And rejoice in You as my God and Savior,
My Jesus

So I open my heart to You right now
        And From the arms of Mary I receive
You into my heart to be my personal Savior,
        My very own Lord and Master.
Take over my life, and make me into the person
        You want me to be. Change me, teach me,
        protect me so that all my thoughts and
        words and actions will be done according to
        Your Spirit.

Thank You for dying on the cross for me,
        And giving up Your Virgin-born Body
        And Blood so that my sins are washed away
        No more remembered against me.
And thank You for promising You will never leave
me
With the help of Your grace I will never leave You.

Thank You, Jesus. Thank You Mary.
Amen
        -- Fr. Philip Pavich, O.F.M., St. James Church
        based on Our Lady's Message of Dec. 25, 1987

TO THE BLESSED VIRGIN

My Queen, My Mother, I give myself entirely to Thee, and to show my devotion to Thee, I consecrate to Thee this day, my eyes, my ears, my mouth, my heart, my whole being without reserve. Wherefore good Mother as I am Thine Own, keep me, guard me, as Thy property and possession. Amen.

"An Indulgence of 500 Days"

FOR THE ELDERLY

Virgin Mother, Mary, you grew old and must often in your loneliness have remembered the days of Nazareth when Jesus and Joseph were with you. Pray for me, please, when loneliness oppresses me. Teach me to remain ever young in heart and to have faith that God will restore the vigor of youth in the joy of heaven.

HAPPINESS

Happiness is a state of mind that depends entirely on you.

We talk of others "making us happy," but this is seldom the case.

We make ourselves happy or unhappy by our attitudes towards ourselves, our work, our neighbors, our world.

The truly happy person is one who can be enthusiastic about the things he or she has to do as well as the things he or she wants to do.

Happiness is a wonderful thing.

It is the one gift we can give ourselves – and the most precious gift we can wish for others.

A farmer placed a weather vane atop his barn. It bore the inscription "God Is Love." Does that mean," a neighbor asked, "that God is fickle as the wind?" "Not in the least," replied the farmer, "It means that God is Love no matter which way the winds is blowing."

HOLY WATER

God Himself prescribed the use of water for His people as a rite of purification (Book of Numbers, 19). Holy water is a sacramental that remits venial sin. The devil hates holy water because of its power over him. He cannot abide long in a place or near a person that is often sprinkled with this blessed water. It is recommended that a parent sprinkle each bedroom with holy water each night before going to bed. The holy souls in purgatory long for holy water. Never forget them at the holy water front. The holy souls nearest to Heaven may need the sprinkling of only one drop to release them from Purgatory. So many benefits from holy water and we give it so little thought!

OTHERS

Lord, help me live from day to day
   In such a self-forgetful way,
That even when I kneel to pray,
   My prayer shall be for "Others."
Help me in all the work I do
   To ever be sincere and true,
And know, that all I do for You
   Must needs be done for "Others."
And when my work on earth is done,
And my new work in Heaven's begun,
May I forget the crown I've won,
   While thinking still of "Others."
"Others," Lord, yes, "Others!"
   Let this my motto be.
Help me to live for others
   That I may live for Thee.

"Feelings are not facts.
Once you've asked for God's forgiveness,
He forgives and forgets."

"Sometimes God has to
        allow trouble in our
lives before we will seek
        him. Multitudes of
people never begin to
        think of their sins or of
their need of salvation
        until the hour of pain,
sickness, bereavement
        or death."

You can do this right now through prayer – which is simply talking with God. God knows your heart and is not so concerned with your words as He is with the attitude of your heart. The following is a suggested prayer:

"Lord Jesus, I have tried to run my life on my own. Please forgive me. I realize I need You. I open the door of my life and receive You as my Saviour and Lord. Take control of the throne of my life. Make me the kind of person You want me to be. Thank you for dying on the cross so that I could be forgiven. Thank you for eternal life."

Does this prayer express the desire of your heart? If it does, now is the time to ask Christ to come into your life.

29

PHILOSOPHY OF LIFE

I was created, like all other things, for the honor and glory of God. God wished to reproduce some of His own perfection in me, that my existence might be life an everlasting evidence of His power, intelligence, and freedom. To God, man is the pinnacle of His creation – the ultimate expression of divine ingenuity. Man is the only creature on earth to whom God gave the privilege of freely honoring Him.

Resolve to love God with your whole heart, whole soul, whole mind, and whole strength, and your neighbor as yourself – or better still, as Christ loves you. Count no sacrifice too great that you are called upon to make in order to avoid hell. Do not allow short lives pleasures that the world, the flesh and the devil offer you, to betray you and make you forgetful of the real purpose of your life on earth.

Doing the will of God to prove our love still is the greatest act a person can perform. God alone knows all the good you do and all the evil you avoid. Happiness does not come from doing what we like to do, but from liking what we have to do. Happiness comes from within ourselves. Life is long, hard and dull – but a just trial determining all eternity. We are on their earth for one reason: to win our salvation. Nothing else really matters.

MEDITATION

I am the Light, and you do not see me.

I am the Way, and you do not follow me.

I am the Truth, and you do not believe me.

I am the Life, and you do not seek me.

I am the Mater, and you do not listen to me.

I am the Chief, and you do not obey.

I am your God, and you do not pray to me.

I am the Best Friend, and you do not live me.

If you are unhappy, do not blame me!

THERE'S A REASON

For every pain, that we must bear,
For every burden, every care,
　　There's a reason.

For every grief, that bows the head,
For every teardrop that is shed,
　　There's a reason.

For every hurt, for every plight,
For every lonely, pain racked night,
　　There's a reason.

But if we trust God, as we should,
It will all work out for our good,
　　He knows the reason.

IF GOD SHOULD GO ON STRIKE

How good it is that God above
        has never gone on strike,
Because He was not treated fair
        in things He didn't like.
If only once, He'd given up and
        said, "That's it. I'm through.
I've had enough of those on Earth
        so this is what I'll do:
I'll give my orders to the sun
        cut off the heat supply!
And to the moon – give no more light,
        and run the oceans dry.
Then just to make things really tough
        and put the pressure on,
Turn off the vital oxygen till
        every breath is gone!"
You know He would be justified
        if fairness was the game,
For no one has been more abused
        or met with more disdain
Than God, and yet He carries on,
        supplying you and me
With all the favors of His grace,
        and everything for free.
Men say they want a better deal,
        and so on strike they go,
But what a deal we've given God
        to whom all things we owe.
We don't care whom we hurt
        to gain the things we like;
But what a mess we'd all be in
        if God should go on strike.

BE SATISFIED

Be satisfied with what you have,
      Thank God for what is yours,
The Lord walks close beside you,
      As long as time endures.
The bitter disappointments,
      He will gently brush away,
His loving arms will hold you close,

      Forever and a day.
You need not ever worry
      That He will not understand,
Or that He'll push you from Him
      With a cold and careless hand.
For He knows our deepest longings,
      And the tears we try to hide,
And His love is deep and lasting
      And His arms are open wide.

GOD'S BOUQUET

You must bloom where you are planted
     In the garden we call life,
And bring some special beauty to
     Each corner where there's strife.

Perhaps you're but a dandelion,
     Wishing you were a rose,
Yet in this place of growing things,
     You're the one God chose.

It's up to you to finish what
     The Good Lord has begun,
By growing just the way you should
     And face the rising sun.

There's room for you, if you but choose,
     In a glorious array
Of beauty from God's garden, that
     He'll add to His bouquet.

-- Sister Miriam Barker, C.D.S.

34

PRAYER FOR A FAMILY

O dear Jesus,
> I humbly implore You to grant Your special graces to our family. May our home be the shrine of peace, purity, love, labor and faith. I beg You, dear Jesus, to protect and bless all of us, absent and present, living and dead.

O Mary,
> Loving Mother of Jesus, and our Mother, pray to Jesus for our family, for all the families of the world, to guard the cradle of the newborn, the schools of the young and their vocations.

Blessed Saint Joseph,
> Holy guardian of Jesus and Mary, assist us by your prayers in all necessities of life. Ask of Jesus that special grace which He granted to you, to watch over our home at the pillow of the sick and the dying, so that with Mary and with you, heaven may find our family unbroken in the Sacred Heart of Jesus.
> Amen

"God is gracious.
He wants us to pray, and
He years for us to
Draw new to Him"

"Do not let your heart be troubled. Have faith in God and faith in me. In my Father's house there are many dwelling places; otherwise, how could I have told you that I was going to prepare a place for you? I am indeed going to prepare a place for you, and then I shall come back to take you with me, that where I am you also may be."

YOU ARE LOVED

While on earth, Jesus healed all who sought His help. Now from heaven He continues to send His healing love to help us in our hours of pain, loneliness, sorrow and illness. The heavier the Cross, the more we need his help up Calvary's Hill.

ADORATION

Oh God, why have You created me, why do You create me at this moment? Where are You leading me? Lord, You are more present to me than I to myself, more aware of me than I am of myself. You want to grant me more clarity, but You will not do it without me. You want to give me more awareness, but it is up to me to become aware. You want to give me more love, but, of course, I must respond to Your love.

Adoration is an awareness; an illumination from the higher awareness of God. The spark which we are finds its source in the secret fire of the Love Creator. All of that is less an awareness than a state; the happy state of the creature.

We are not a prison. God has created us with a window, wide open for Him. We are free persons, open to God and to others, that is to say, to Love. The creator Love is poured forth in love for His creatures, and draws us into the same adventure of universal salvation of which we will find the secret in God. This secret of love is the source of all the others.

"My God, I love Thee"
(The best and shortest prayer."

37

PRAYER FOR THE DEAD

God our Father, Your power brings us to birth, Your providence guides our lives, and by Your command we must return to dust.

I pray for the dead, especially for *N*. May tose who have been dear to me in life find a place with You in heaven.

Lord, those who die still live in Your presence; their lives change but do not end. I pray in hope for my family, relatives and friends, and for all the dead known to You alone.

In company with Christ who died and now ives may they rejoice in Your kingdom where all our tears are wiped away. Unite us together again as one family, to sing Your praise forever and ever.

A PRAYER FOR THOSE GROWING OLD

Father, help me to accept the lessening of my powers with realism and good humor.

Keep me from self-pity, and remind me that age has not taken away my mission in life, but only altered it.

Grant me a taste for the hidden beauties of creation, a continuing interest in Your world – and mine.

Make me more patient with myself, more tolerant of the foibles of others, more outgoing with the timid and shy.

Bestow on me a greater readiness for prayer, and a humble acceptance of suffering.

Deepen my faith in Your unfailing truth, strengthen my hope that I will share in the joy of Your Son's resurrection, expand my love in Your Holy Spirit for all men – with whom I am destined to share the fellowship of the blessed for all eternity.

Amen.

People are often the carpenters of their own crosses
-- St. Philip Neri

ST. GERTUDE THE GREAT NOVENA

Lord, increase in us Your gifts of mercy and forgiveness, You showed Your signs of love in the honor you gave St. Gertrude. Lord hear the prayers of those who recall the devoted life of St. Gertrude. Guide us on our way and help us to grow in love and devotion as long as we live.

PRAYER OF ST. GERTRUDE THE GREAT

Dictated by our Lord to release 1,000 Souls from Purgatory each time it is said

"Eternal Father, I offer Thee the Most Precious Blood of Thy Divine Son, Jesus, in union with the Masses said throughout the world today, for all the holy Souls in Purgatory, for sinners everywhere, for sinners in the Universal Church, those in my own home and within my family. Amen."

TO THE HOLY SOULS IN PURGATORY

Oh Holy Spirit, You are the Third Person of the Blessed Trinity! You are the Spirit of truth, love and holiness, proceeding from the Father and the Son, and equal to Them in all things! I adore You and love You with all my heart. Teach me to know and to seek God, by whom and for whom I was created. Fill my heart with a holy fear and a great love of Him. Give me compunction and patience, and do not let me fall into sin.

Increase faith, hope and charity in me and bring forth in me all virtues proper to my state of life. Help me to grow in the four cardinal virtues, Your seven gifts and Your twelve fruits.

Make me a faithful follower of Jesus, an obedient child of the Church and a help to my neighbor. Give me the grace to keep the commandments and to receive the sacraments worthily. Raise me to holiness in the state of life to which You have called me, and lead me through a happy death to everlasting life. Through Jesus Christ, our Lord.

Grant me also, O Holy Spirit, Giver of all good gifts, the special favor for which I ask (*name it*), if it be for Your honor and glory and for my well-being.

Glory be to the Father...

NOVENA PRAYER TO ST. PHILOMENA

O Faithful Virgin and glorious martyr, St. Philomena, who works so many miracles on behalf of the poor and sorrowing, have pity on me. Thou knowest the multitude and diversity of my needs. Behold me at thy feet, full of misery, but full of hope. I entreat thy charity, O great Saint! Graciously hear me and obtain from God a favorable answer to the request which I now humbly lay before thee… (*Here specify your petition.*) I am firmly convinced that through thy merits, through the scorn, the sufferings and the death thou didst endure, united to the merits of the Passion and death of Jesus, thy Spouse, I shall obtain what I ask of thee, and in the joy of my heart I will bless God, who is admirable in His Saints. Amen.

Imprimatur: Carolus Hubertus Le Blond
Episcopus Sancti Josephi
January, 1952

TO ST. PEREGRINE "THE CANCER SAINT"

Glorious wonder-worker, St. Peregrine, you answered the divine call with a ready spirit, and forsook all the comforts of a life of ease and all the empty honors of the world to dedicate yourself to God in the Order of His holy Mother. You labored manfully for the salvation of souls. In union with Jesus crucified, you painful sufferings with such patience as to deserve to be healed miraculously of an incurable cancer in your leg by a touch of His divine hand. Obtain for me the grace to answer every call of God and to fulfil His will in all the events of life. Enkindle in my heart a consuming zeal for the salvation of all men. Deliver me from the infirmities that afflict my body (*especially…*). Obtain for me also a perfect resignation to the sufferings it may please God to send me, so that, imitating our crucified Savior and His sorrowful Mother, I may merit eternal glory in heaven.

St. Peregrine, pray for me and for all who invoke your aid.

It is a very great poverty to decide that a child must die that you might live as you wish. Mother Theresa of Calcutta

PRAYER TO ONE'S PATRON OR ANY SAINT

Glorious Saint N. (my beloved patron), you served God in humility and confidence on earth. Now you enjoy His beatific vision in heaven. You persevered till death and gained the crown of eternal life. Remember now the dangers and confusion and anguish that surround me and intercede for me in my needs and troubles, especially…

Amen.

THE BEST THINGS IN LIFE ARE FREE

When we count
Our many blessings;
It isn't hard to see
That Life's most valued treasures
Are the treasures that are free.

For it isn't what we own or buy
That signified our wealth.
It's the special gifts
That have no price;
Our family, friends and health

TO ST. MICHAEL THE ARCHANGEL

Glorious St. Michael guardian and defender of the Church of Jesus Christ, come to the assistance of His followers, against whom the powers of hell are unchained. Guard with special care our Holy Father, the Pope, and our bishops, priests, all our religious and lay people and especially the children.

St. Michael, watch over us during life, defend us against the assaults of the demon, and assist us especially at the hour of death. Help us achieve th happiness of beholding God face to face for all eternity. Amen.

St. Michael, interceded for me with God in all my necessities, especially (*name it*). Obtain for me a favorable outcome in the matter I recommend to you. Mighty prince of the heavenly host, and victor over rebellious spirits, remember me for I am weak and sinful and so prone to pride and ambition. Be for me, I pray, my powerful aid in temptation and difficulty, and above all do not forsake me in my last struggle with the powers of evil. Amen.

A day hemmed in prayer is less likely to unravel

TO ST. RAPHAEL THE ARCHANGEL

Glorious Archangel St. Raphael, great prince of
the heavenly court, you are illustrious for your gifts
of wisdom and grace. You are a guide of those
who journey by land or sea or air, consoler of the
afflicted, and refuge of sinners. I beg you, assist
me in all my needs and in all the sufferings of this
life, as once you helped the young Tobias on his
travels. Because you are the "medicine of God," I
humbly pray you to heal the many infirmities of my
soul and the ills that afflict by body. I especially
ask of you the favor (*name it*) and the great gace
of purity to prepare me to be the temple of the
Holy Spirit. Amen.

> St. Raphael, of the glorious seven
> who stand
> Before the throne of Him who lives
> and reigns.
> Angel of health, the Lord has filled
> your hand
> With balm from heaven to soothe
> or cure our pains.
> Heal or cure the victim of disease.
> And guide our steps when doubtful
> of our ways.

TO GOOD ST. ANNE

Glorious St. Anne, we think of you and with compassion for those who invoke you and with love for those who suffer. Heavily laden with the weight of my troubles, I cast myself at your feet and humbly beg of you to take the present affair which I commend to you under your special protection (name it).

Deign to commend it to your daughter, our Blessed Lady, and lay it before the throne of Jesus, so that He may bring it to a happy conclusion. Cease not to intercede for me until my request is granted. Above all, obtain for me the grace of one day beholding my God face to face. With you and Mary and all the saints, may I praise and bless Him for all eternity. Amen.

Good St. Anne, mother of her who is our life, our sweetness and our hope, pray for me.

PRAYER TO ST. ANTHONY

O Holy St. Anthony, gentlest of Saints, your love
for God and charity for His creatures made you
worthy when on earth to possess miraculous
powers. Miracles waited on your word, which
you were ever ready to speak for those in trouble
or anxiety. Encouraged by this thought, I Implore
you to obtain for me … (*Here mention your
request.*) The answer to my prayer may require a
miracle; even so, you are the Saint of Miracles.
O gentle and loving St. Anthony whose heart
was ever full of human sympathy, whisper my
petition into the ears of the sweet Infant Jesus,
who loved to be folded in your arms, and the
gratitude of my heart will ever be yours. Amen

St. Anthony of Padua is involved in a wide
variety of needs but is especially renowned as
the "Patron of Lost Objects."

*"Ask, and it shall be given you; seek, and you
shall find; knock, and it shall be opened to you.
For every on that asketh, receiveth; and he the
seeketh, findeth; and to him that knocketh, it
shall be opened."*

                              -- Matthew 7:7-8

TO ST. GERARD

For an expectant Mother

Great St. Gerard, beloved servant of Jesus Christ, you are a perfect imitator for our meek and humble Savior, and a devoted child of the Mother of God. Enkindle in my heart of spark of that heavenly fire of Charity that glowed in yours and made you a beacon of Love.

Glorious St. Gerard, like your divine Master you bore without murmur or complaint the calumnies of wicked men when falsely accused of crime, and you have been raised up by God as the patron and protector of expectant mothers. Preserve me from dangers, and shield the child I now carry. Pray that my baby may be brought safely to the light of day and receive the sacrament of baptism.

Hail, Mary...

TO ST. GERARD

For motherhood or for some other special favor

*(St. Gerard is also invoked as the patron of a
Good confession.)*

Most Blessed Trinity, I, Your child, thank you for
all the gifts and privileges which you granted to
St. Gerard, especially for those virtues with
which You adorned him on earth and the glory
which You now impart to him in heaven.
Accomplish your work, Oh Lord, so that Your
kingdom may come about on earth. Through his
merits, in union with those of Jesus and Mary,
grant me the grace for which I ask...

And you, my powerful intercessor, St. Gerard,
always so ready to help those who have
recourse to you, pray for me. Come before the
throne of Divine Mercy and do not leave without
being heard. To you I confide this important and
urgent affair... Graciously take my cause in hand
and do not let me end this novena without
having experienced in some way the effects of
your intercession. Amen.

TO ST. DYMPHNA

For the mentally afflicted

O God, we humbly beseech You through Your servant, St. Dymphna, who sealed with her blood the love she bore You, to grant relief to those who suffer from mental afflictions and nervous disorders, especially...

St. Dymphna, helper of the mentally afflicted, pray for us.

Glory be to the Father...

Seven days without Jesus makes one weak.

TO ST. MARY GORETTI

St. Mary Goretti, strengthened by God's grace, you did not hesitate, even at the age of eleven, to sacrifice life itself to defend your virginal purity. Look graciously on the unhappy human race that has strayed far from the path of eternal salvation. Teach us all, and especially our youth, the courage and promptness that will help us avoid anything that could offend Jesus. Obtain for me a great horror of sin, so that I may live a holy life on earth and win eternal glory in heaven. *Amen.*

Our Father, Hail, Mary, Glory be.

TO ST. THERESE OF THE CHILD JESUS, "THE LITTLE FLOWER"

I greet you, St. Therese of the Child Jesus, lily of purity, ornament and glory of Christianity. I greet you, great Saint, seraph of divine love. I rejoice at the favors our blessed Lord Jesus has liberally bestowed on you. In humility and confidence, I ask you to help me, for I know that God has given you love and pity as well as power. Then, behold my distress, my anxiety, my fears. Tell Him my wants. Your requests will crown my petition with success, will fill me with joy, remember your promise to do good on earth. Please obtain for me from God the graces I hope for from the infinite goodness of our blessed Lord, especially ... Amen.

TO THE HOLY ANGELS

Bless the Lord, all you His angels. You who are mighty in strength and do His will, intercede for me at the throne of God. By your unceasing watchfulness protect me in every danger of soul and body. Obtain for me the grace of final perseverance, so that after this life I may be admitted to your glorious company and with you may sing the praises of God for all eternity.

All you holy angels and archangels, thrones and dominations, principalities and powers and virtues of heaven, cherubim and seraphim, and especially you, my dear guardian angel, intercede for me and obtain for me the special favor I now ask *(mention it)*.

Glory to be the Father ...

NOVENA TO ST. JOSEPH

Glorious St. Joseph, foster-father and protector of Jesus Christ! To you I raise my heart and my hands to implore your powerful intercession. Please obtain for me from the kind Heart of Jesus the help and the graces necessary for my spiritual and temporal welfare. I ask particularly for the grace of a happy death and the special favor I now implore *(name it)*.

Guardian of the Word Incarnate, I feel animated with confidence that your prayers in my behalf will be graciously heard before the throne of God.

V. O glorious St. Joseph, through the love you bear to Jesus Christ, and for the glory of His name,

R. Hear my prayers and obtain my petitions.

TO OUR LADY OF PERPETUAL HELP

Oh Mother of perpetual Help, grant that I may
ever invoke your powerful name, the protection
of the living and the salvation of the dying.
Purest Mary, let your name henceforth be ever
on my lips. Delay not, Blessed Lady, to rescue
me whenever I call on you. In my temptations, in
my needs, I will never cease to call on you, ever
repeating your sacred name, Mary, Mary. What
a consolation, what sweetness, what confidence
fills my soul when I utter your sacred name or
even only think of you! I thank the Lord for
having given you so sweet, so powerful, so
lovely a name. But I will not be content with
merely uttering your name. Let my love for you
prompt me ever to hail you Mother of Perpetual
Help.

Mother of Perpetual Help, pray for me and grant
me the favor I confidently ask you.

Hail Mary …

PRAYER TO ST. PIUS X

Glorious Pope of the Eucharist, St. Pius X, you sought "to restore all things in Christ." Obtain for me a true love of Jesus so that I may live only for Him. Help me to acquire a lively fervor and a sincere will to strive for sanctity of life, and that I may avail myself of the riches of the Holy Eucharist in sacrifice and sacrament. By your love for Mary, mother and queen of all, inflame my heart with tender devotion to her.

NOVENA OF GRACE IN HONOR OF ST. FRANCIS XAVIER

Great St. Francis, well beloved and full of charity, in union with you I reverently adore the Divine Majesty. I give thanks to God for the singular gifts of grace bestowed on you in life and of glory after death, and I beg to you, with all the affection of my heart, by your powerful intercession, obtain for me the grace to live a holy life and die a holy death, I beg to you to obtain (here mention special spiritual or temporal favors); but if what I ask in not the glory of God and for my well-being, obtain for me, I beseech you, what will more certainly attain these ends. Amen.

Our Father, Hail, Mary, Glory be.

NOVENA TO ST. RITA

Helper of the hopeless

Holy Patroness of those in need, St. Rita, you were humble, pure and patient. Your pleadings with your divine Spouse are irresistible, so please obtain for me from our risen Jesus the request I make of you (mention it). Be kind to me for the greater glory of God, and I shall honor you and sing your praises forever.

Glorious St. Rita, you miraculously participated in the sorrowful passion of our Lord Jesus Christ. Obtain for me now the grace to suffer with resignation the troubles of this life, and protect me in all my needs. Amen.

Our Father, Hail, Mary, Glory be to the Father…

TO OUR LADY OF LOURDES

Oh ever immaculate Virgin, Mother of Mercy, Health of the Sick, Refuge of Sinners. Comfortress of the Afflicted, you know my wants, my troubles, my sufferings. Look upon me with mercy. When you appeared in the grotto of Lourdes you made it a privileged sanctuary where you dispense your favors, and where many sufferers have obtained the cure of their infirmities, both spiritual and corporal. I come, therefore, with unbounded confidence to implore your maternal intercession. My loving Mother, obtain my request. I will try to imitate your virtues so that I may one day share your company and bless you in eternity. Amen.

TO ST. BENEDICT

Glorious St. Benedict, sublime model of virtue, pure vessel of God's grace! Behold me humbly kneeling at your feet. I implore you in your loving kindness to pray for me before the throne of God. To you I have recourse in the dangers that daily surround me. Shield me against my selfishness and my indifference to God and to my neighbor. Inspire me to imitate you in all things. May your blessing be with me always, so that I may see and serve Christ in others and work for His kingdom.

Graciously obtain for me from God those favors and graces which I need so much in the trials, miseries and afflictions of life. Your heart was always full of love, compassion and mercy toward those who were afflicted or troubled in any way. You never dismissed without consolation and assistance anyone who had recourse to you. I therefore invoke your powerful intercession, confident in the hope that you will hear my prayers and obtain for me the special grace and favor I earnestly implore (name it).

Help me, great St. Benedict, to live and die as a faithful child of God, to run in the sweetness of His loving will and to attain the eternal happiness of heaven. Amen.

TO ST. ANTHONY MARY CLARET

Helper of those suffering from cancer, heart trouble, and other serious ailments of soul and body.

St. Anthony Mary Claret, during your life on earth you often comforted the afflicted and showed such tender love and compassion for the sick and sinful. Intercede for me now that you rejoice in the reward of your virtues in heavenly glory. Look with pity on me (or on the person afflicted or whose conversion is desired) and grant my prayer, if such be the will of God. Make my troubles your own. Speak a word for me to the Immaculate Heart of Mary to obtain by her powerful intercession the grace I yearn for so ardently, and a blessing to strengthen me during life, assist me at the hour of death, and lead me to a happy eternity. Amen

PRAYER TO BE SAID BY A SICK PERSON

O Merciful Infant Jesus! I know of Your miraculous deeds for the sick. How many diseases You cured during Your blessed life on earth, and how many venerators of Your Miraculous image ascribe to You their recovery and deliverance from most painful and hopeless maladies. I know, indeed, that a sinner like me has merited his sufferings and has no right to ask for favors. But in view of the innumerable graces and the miraculous cures granted even to the greatest sinners through the veneration of Your holy infancy, particularly in the miraculous statue of Prague or in representations of it, I exclaim with the greatest assurance: O most loving Infant Jesus, full of pity, You can cure me if You will. Do not hesitate, O Heavenly Physician, if it be Your will that I recover from this present illness; extend Your most holy hands, and by Your power take away all pain and infirmity, so that my recovery may be due, not to natural remedies, but to You alone. If, however, You in Your inscrutable wisdom have determined otherwise, then at least restore my soul to perfect health, and fill me with heavenly consolation and blessing, that I may be like You, O Jesus, in my sufferings, and may glorify Your providence until, at the death of my body, You bestow on me eternal life. Amen.

IN HONOR OF THE SORROWSOF THE BLESSSED VIRGIN MARY

Most holy and afflicted Virgin, Queen of Martyrs, you stood beneath the cross, witnessing the agony of your dying Son. Look with a mother's tenderness and pity on me, who kneel before you. I venerate your sorrows and I place my requests with filial confidence in the sanctuary of your wounded heart.

Present them, I beseech you, on my behalf to Jesus Christ, through the merits of His own most sacred passion and death, together with your sufferings at the foot of the cross. Through the united efficacy of both, obtain the granting of my petition. To whom shall I have recourse in my wants and miseries if not to you, Mother of Mercy? You have drunk so deeply of the chalice of your Son, you can compassionate our sorrows.

Holy Mary, your soul was pierced by a sword of sorrow at the sight of the passion of your divine Son. Intercede for me and obtain for me from Jesus (mention the desired favor) if it be for His honor and glory and for my good. Amen.

TO ST. LUCY

St. Lucy, your beautiful name signifies light. By the light of faith which God bestowed upon you, increase and preserve this light in my soul so that I may avoid evil, be zealous in the performance of good works, and abhor nothing so much as the blindness and the darkness of evil and of sin.

By your intercession with God, obtain for me perfect vision for my bodily eyes and the grace to use them for God's greater honor and glory and the salvation of all men.

St. Lucy, virgin and martyr, hear my prayers and obtain my petitions. Amen.

TO ST. JUDE THE APOSTLE

Glorious Apostle, St. Jude Thaddeus, I salute you through the Sacred Heart of Jesus. Through His Heart I praise and thank God for all the graces He has bestowed upon you. I implore you, through His love to look upon me with compassion. Do not despise my poor prayer. Do not let my trust be confounded! God has granted to you the privilege of aiding mankind in the most desperate cases. Oh, come to my aid that I may praise the mercies of God. All my life I will be your grateful client until I can thank you in heaven. Amen.

St. Jude, pray for us,

And for all who invoke your aid.

NOVENA OF CONFIDENCE TO THE
SACRED HEART

Oh Lord Jesus Christ, to Your most Sacred Heart I confide this intention (your request). Only look upon me, then do what Your love inspires, Let Your Sacred Heart decide... I count on You...I trust in You... I throw myself on Your mercy. Lord Jesus. You will not fail me.

Sacred Heart of Jesus, I trust in You.

Sacred Heart of Jesus, I believe in Your love for me.

Sacred Heart of Jesus, Your kingdom come.

Sacred Heart of Jesus, I have asked You for many favors, but I earnestly implore this one. Take it, place it in Your open Heart. When the Eternal Father looks upon it, He will see it. Jesus, You said, "Heaven and earth shall pass away, but My word shall not pass." Through the intercession of Mary, Your holy Mother, I feel confident that my prayer will be granted.

Mention your request.

God give work till my life shall end and life till my work is done.

NOVENA PRAYERS TO OUR LADY OF THE SNOWS

Remember, O most gracious Virgin Mary, that never was it known that anyone who fled to thy protection, implored thy help or sought thy intercession, was left unaided. Inspired with this confidence, I fly unto thee, O Virgin of virgins, my Mother; to thee do I come, before thee I stand, sinful and sorrowful; O Mother of the Word Incarnate, despise not my petitions, but in thy mercy hear and answer me. Amen.

Our Father Hail Mary
Our Lady of the Snows, pray for us.
St. Joseph, pray for us.
St. Therese, The Little Flower, pray for us.
Glory Be to the Father, etc.

NOVENA IN URGENT NEED TO THE INFANT JESUS OF PRAGUE

To be said for nine consecutive hours or for nine days

Jesus, You said, "Ask and you shall receive, seek and you shall find, knock and it shall be opened to you." Through the intercession of Mary, Your holy Mother, I knock, I seek, I ask that my prayer be granted.

Mention your request.

Jesus, You said, "All that you ask of the Father in My name, He will grant you." Through the intercession of Mary, Your holy Mother, I humbly and urgently ask Your Father in Your name that my prayer be granted.

Mention your request.

Jesus, You said, "Heaven and earth shall pass away, but My word shall not pass." Through the intercession of Mary, Your holy Mother, I feel confident that my prayer will be granted.

Mention your request.

THE BOOK OF LIFE!

If you would like to know God, look at the Crucifix!

If you would like to LOVE GOD, LOOK AT the Crucifix

If you want to serve God, look at the Crucifix!

If you wonder how much God loves you, look at the Crucifix!

If you wonder how much He wants you in heaven, look at the Crucifix!

If you wonder how He tries to prevent you from the yawning jaws of hell, look at the Crucifix!

If you wonder how much He will help you to save your immortal soul, look at the Crucifix!

If you wonder how much you should forgive others, look at the Crucifix!

If you wonder how much your faith demands of you, i n humility, poverty, charity, meekness, and every virtue, look at the Crucifix!

If you want to know what unselfishness and generosity are, look at the Crucifix!

If you wonder how far your own unselfishness should go to bring others to Christ, look at the Crucifix!

If you want to understand the need for self-denial and mortification, look at the Crucifix!

If you wish to live well, look at the Crucifix!

If you wish to die well, look at the Crucifix!

GREAT THOUGHTS

ETERNITY

O Mortal, who hast an immortal soul, study, meditate upon, thoroughly realize that great word

ETERNITY!

I may reckon upon a thousand years, ten thousand years, a hundred million times a thousand years, so many millions of times a thousand years as there are

Leaves on the trees of the forest,
Blades of grass in the fields,
Grains of sand on the seashore,
Drops of water in the ocean,
Stars in the sky:

And I will not yet have begun to tell what thou art,

O ETERNITY!

YOUR CROSS

The everlasting God has in His wisdom foreseen from eternity the cross that He now presents to you as a gift from His inmost Heart.

This cross He now sends you He has considered with His all-knowing eyes, understood with His Divine mind, tested with His wise justice, warmed with loving arms and weighed with His own hands to see that it be not one inch too large and not one ounce too heavy for you. He has blessed it with His holy Name, anointed it with His grace, perfumed it with His consolation, taken one last glance at you and your courage, and then sent it to you from Heaven, a special greeting from God to you, an alms of the all-merciful love of God.

-- St. Francis de Sales

ANGEL'S PRAYER

With the Blessed Sacrament suspended in the air, the angel at Fatima prostrated himself, and recited this prayer:

O Most Holy Trinity, Father, Son and Holy Spirit, I adore Thee profoundly. I offer Thee the most precious Body, Blood, Soul and Divinity of Jesus Christ, present in all the tabernacles of the world, in reparation for the outrages, sacrileges and indifference by which He is offended. By the infinite merits of the Sacred Heart of Jesus and the Immaculate Heart of Mary. I beg the conversion of poor sinners.

On Calvary there was one man brave enough to die and one woman brave enough to go on living; so all men may know that life and death demand the same ingredient of courage.
-- Walter Farrell

"HONOR THY FATHER..."

that it may be well thee...

"Lord teach us to pray." St. Luke 11:1.

Our Father, who art in heaven, hallowed be Thy name. Thy kingdom come; Thy will be done on earth, as it is in heaven. Give us this day our daily bread; and forgive us our trespasses, as we forgive those who trespass against us. And lead us not into temptation but deliver us from evil. Amen.

"Pray to Thy Father in secret; and Thy Father who seeth in secret will repay thee."

-- St. M t. 6:6.

"He who prays shall be saved, he who prays not shall be condemned."

-- St. Alphonsus de Liguori.

The bad thief on the cross will confess on the day of judgment concerning the good thief; "He was not less guilty than I, yet he ascended from his cross into heaven, while I from mine was hurled into hell, because I neglected to pray."

-- Fr. Michael Mueller.

"All those who burn in hell either did not pray or did not pray enough. God has tied up salvation to this very easy thing."

-- Cry of a Lost Soul.

THE HEART OF CHRIST

Come to me, all of you
Who are weary and
find life burdensome;
I will refresh you.
Take my yoke on your shoulders
and learn from me,
for I am gentle and humble of heart.
You shall find rest
because my yoke is easy and burden light.

--Mathew 11:28-30

THE LEGEND OF THE DOGWOOD

There is a legend that at the time of the crucifixion the dogwood had been the size of the oak and other forest trees. So firm and strong was the tree that it was chosen as the timber for the cross. To be used for such a cruel purpose greatly distressed the tree, and our Lord, nailed upon it, sensed this, and in his gentle pity for all sorrow and suffering said to it: "Because of your regret and pity for my suffering, never again shall the dogwood tree grow large enough to be used as a cross. Henceforth it shall be slender and bent and twisted, and its blossoms shall be in the form of a cross, two long and two short petals. And in the center of the outer edge of each petal there will be nail prints, brown with rust and stained with red, and in the center of the flower will be a crown of thorns, and all who see it will remember."

To give and not to count the cost; to fight and not to heed the wounds; to toil and not to seek for rest; to labor and not ask for reward save knowing that we do Thy will.

-- St. Ignatius

STAYING CLOSE TO JESUS

Lord, Jesus, I pray in remembrance of Your suffering in the garden of Gethsemane.

I place myself there with You in Your time of need.

I share Your sorrow and beg forgiveness for the sins of mankind, the source of Your agony.

Thank you, Jesus, for Your love for me, for Your Sacrifice for my redemption.

Lord Jesus, please be here in my times of need.

Without Your grace, Your presence, I cannot succeed in my own agony in the garden.

Please be my comfort and my strength.

♦♦♦♦♦♦♦♦♦♦

Every human being is entirely unique.

Out of all the billions of people in this world, there is not one who is an exact carbon copy of you.

There is no one with exactly the same characteristics and attitudes, the same kind of temperament and personality.

In God's providence you are made unique in this way.

You are meant to reach out and touch certain hearts, in a way that no one else can reach them and touch them.

There is a special task for which you have been chosen by God.

LORD, TAKE MY WILL

I'll go where you want me to go, dear Lord,
Over mountains, or valley, or sea;
I' II say what you want 1ne to say, dear Lord,
I'll be what you want me to be.
It may not be on the mountain height
Or over the stormy sea;
It may not be at the battle's front
My Lord will have need of me;
But if by a still small voice He calls
To paths that I do not know,
I'll answer, dear Lord, with my hand in yours,
I'll go where you want me to go.

A PRAYER TO REDEEM LOST TIME

by St. Teresa of Avila

O My God! Source of all mercy! I acknowledge
Your sovereign power. While recalling the
wasted years that are past, I believe that You,
Lord, can in an instant turn this loss to gain.
Miserable as I am, yet I firmly believe that You
can do all things. Please restore to me the time
lost, giving me Your grace, both now and in the
future, that I may appear before You in "wedding
garments." Amen

"Let the little children come to me. Do not shut them off. The reign of God belongs to such as these. Trust me when I tell you that whoever does not accept the kingdom of God as a child will not enter into it."
(Luke 18: 16-17)

Keep working for the Lord -
the pay isn't much but...
"the benefits and retirement
plan is out of this world."